INSTANT ACTIVITIES
for
POETRY
That Kids Really Love!

SCHOLASTIC
PROFESSIONAL **B**OOKS

NEW YORK ◆ TORONTO ◆ LONDON ◆ AUCKLAND ◆ SYDNEY

Edited by Linda Beech. Written by Merrily P. Hansen,
Marty Lee, Tara McCarthy, and Marcia Miller

Cover design by Vincent Ceci and Jaime Lucero

Cover Illustration by Abby Carter

Interior design by Ellen Matlach Hassell
for Boultinghouse & Boultinghouse, Inc.

Interior illustrations by Teresa Anderko, Delana Bettoli,
Rick Brown, Drew Hires, and Manuel Rivera.

ISBN 0-590-37352-8

CONTENTS

(continued on the next page)

Introduction

Somewhere in our hearts and minds, we all have poetry in us. With this book, *Instant Activities for Poetry That Kids Really Love!*, you and your students can explore together the many possibilities for writing and responding to poems—yours, theirs, other students', and those of many fine and established poets.

An intriguing way to begin is with the poster that accompanies this book. The poem on the poster, titled "What If," was written especially for the book by poet Bobbi Katz* to engage students in one of the most important aspects of poetry—the selection of words.

Another poet, Jacqueline Sweeney,** developed the poetry-writing project. It's jam-packed with firsthand tips on how to start, what to do, what materials to use, and how to succeed. As she points out, "Poems are not just for special occasions, but for every day." They are indeed, and *Teaching Poetry* will help you make poetry a part of your curriculum throughout the year. You'll find pages for reading aloud, listening to, and writing many different kinds of poems.

This is a book to skip around in. Though one project is about appreciating poetry and one is on writing poems, as you can see from all the ideas and activities and cross references throughout the book, reading and writing poetry are hopelessly—and deliciously—intertwined. Use the start-up suggestions to create a special poetry place in your classroom, and then bring in the poems and activities as you like to get yor students playing with words and excited about poems.

According to poet James Dickey, "Poetry makes possible the deepest kind of personal possession of the world." We hope that this book provides your class with great pleasure as you explore the endless possibilities for connecting through language.

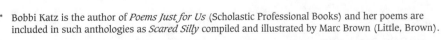

* Bobbi Katz is the author of *Poems Just for Us* (Scholastic Professional Books) and her poems are included in such anthologies as *Scared Silly* compiled and illustrated by Marc Brown (Little, Brown).

** Jacqueline Sweeney is the author of *Quick Poetry Activities You Can Really Do* and *Teaching Poetry: Yes You Can!* (Scholastic Professional Books). Her poetry can be found in many anthologies.

Smart Starts...

...and techniques to use throughout the year

A Poet's Place

What will inspire your young poets? A special place for exploring and writing poetry may be just the thing. Here are some suggestions for setting up a poetry center in your classroom.

Stocking the Center

Set up an area where students can surround themselves with poetry. Display the poster that comes with this book. You might also copy and display page 35, an interview with Bobbi Katz, who wrote the poster poem. Display and store materials in easy reach of the workspace. Some materials to include:

◆ activities and reproducibles; see pages 51–68 (You might place each in a folder, taping a copy to the outside for easy reference.)

◆ assorted poetry books

◆ individual poetry journals or folders

◆ a blank book in which children can paste copies of poems they want to share

◆ markers, paints, construction paper, oak tag, and other materials for illustrating and displaying poems

◆ an atlas (useful for searching for unusual names of places that might become the focus of a poem)

◆ newspapers (a source of poetic inspiration)

◆ a dictionary and a thesaurus

◆ a tape recorder, blank tapes (for recording oral readings), tapes of poetry readings that reflect different voices and cultures

◆ other materials suggested by students

Inspiration Board

Poet Bobbi Katz keeps a bulletin board full of inspiration at home. (See page 35.) Note cards, newspaper clippings, and snapshots are a few of the things that she tacks up. Set aside a bulletin board at the poetry center for students to post articles and images of special interest. Students searching for words, images, and ideas will soon have plenty to choose from!

Punchboard Poetry

A punchboard is a rectangular board with holes, each filled with a message written on a small paper scroll. Players take turns "punching" out scrolls and doing whatever is indicated in the message. Here's how you can create a poetry punchboard and offer students a new experience each time they visit.

1. Cut paper into 5-inch squares.

2. On each slip, write a poetry activity.

3. Roll up each slip of paper and secure it with a "ring" of paper.

4 Stand scrolls side by side in an uncovered shoe box (or other small container).

5. Invite children to "punch" (choose) scrolls with their fingers when they visit the center, then follow the directions.

Sample Poetry Punchboard Activities

◆ Write five words that rhyme with peas. Try putting them together to make a silly poem.

◆ Can you write a poem about popsicles that looks good enough to eat? A poem in the shape of what it's about is called a concrete poem. Try writing concrete poems about other things, like skateboards, snails, and ice cream.

◆ Do you remember a favorite nursery rhyme? Copy it and post it at the center.

Poets' Word Box

In poetry, more than almost any other form of writing, every word counts!

The glossary on this page provides definitions of some key words used to discuss elements of poetry. You may wish to introduce the words as students come across examples of them. Then give students hands-on practice with the activities that follow.

alliteration the repetition of beginning consonant sounds (jingle, jangle, jamboree) (See page 71.)

assonance the repetition of vowel sounds (same, rain, makes, pavement) (See page 43.)

consonance the repetition of consonant sounds anywhere in the words (Carlos wore a black jacket.) (See page 71.)

end rhyme the rhyming of words at the ends of two or more lines of poetry (See page 56.)

free verse poetry that does not include patterned rhyme or rhythm (See poster.)

haiku a three-line Japanese poem about nature; the first line has five syllables; the second, seven; and the third, five. (See page 59.)

imagery pictures that are created with words (See pages 11 and 42.)

limerick a funny verse in five lines. Lines one, two, and five rhyme, as do two and four. (See page 56.)

metaphor a comparison without using the words like or as (See page 27.)

narrative a poem that tells a story (See pages 23–24.)

onomatopoeia words whose sounds make you think of their meanings (See page 30.)

personification a comparison in which something that is not human is described with human characteristics (See page 29.)

repetition the repeating of a word or phrase to add rhythm (See page 36.)

rhythm the pattern of accented and unaccented syllables in a line of poetry (See page 62.)

simile a comparison that uses the words *like* or *as* (See page 25.)

Poetry Word Webs

Challenge students to web these words around common concepts; for example, "The Sounds of Poetry" (alliteration, assonance, consonance), "Figures of Speech" (simile, metaphor), "Forms of Poetry" (ballad, couplet, haiku), and "Poet's Helpers" (rhyming dictionary, thesaurus). As students meet new terms and explore other poetic forms in unit activities, suggest they add these terms to their webs. Students can also play a word web game by filling in everything but the central words. Have them challenge a partner to fill in the missing center of their web.

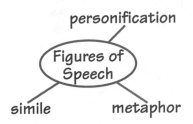

Example, Please

Encourage students to annotate this list of terms with examples drawn from the poems that they explore during this unit. For example, "Packing Up" on page 29 is a good example of personification, and Poe's poem "The Bells" on page 30 illustrates onomatopoeia.

Scrapbook Journals

A poem begins long before it's written down. It often begins with sudden sights and other sensory impressions. No wonder so many poets keep a small journal handy in which to capture those fleeting, vivid impressions. By setting up and keeping scrapbook journals, students will build their sensory awareness and learn to value it as a source of poems that are yet to be.

Format

Like any scrapbook, this one should have big sturdy pages on which students can write, draw, and even paste or glue small items such as photos, feathers, or leaves. A loose-leaf binder is ideal, because students can interleaf it as they go on to the next journaling step. (See next page.)

Introducing the Scrapbook Journal

Choose a time when the class has just returned from some special event, such as a school play, a field trip, or a community project. Explain that a scrapbook journal is a way to "bank" sights, sounds, and other sensory impressions so they won't be forgotten. Ahead of time, set up two or three pages in your own scrapbook journal to use as a model. Head each page with the day's date. Ideally, these pages will record an example

of each of the senses and show objects or pictures as well as written phrases.

Group Practice

Discuss the special event students have just experienced. Focus on what students saw, heard, smelled, tasted, or touched. If the event involved them in movement, such as a school track meet, ask them to brainstorm words about how they felt as they moved. Then have students work in groups of five or six. Give each group a scrapbook journal page and ask them to decide on and record their most vivid sensory impressions, using your pages as a model if they want. Because students will not at this point have objects to paste on the pages, suggest they note what small object they would paste down if they could.

Invite the groups to share their finished pages. As appropriate, comment on scrapbook entries that seem to hold the seeds for a piece of writing and encourage students to make their own comments in this regard.

Going On

Students can now begin their individual scrapbook journals. Ask them to collect sensory impressions to "bank" the next day. Set aside ten minutes or so of class time for "banking." Explain that a student's journal pages will be private, to share or not to share as he or she wishes. Encourage students to use their scrapbook journals at least three times a week.

I found this on the shore. It feels soft.

I saw floating feathers on a silent pond.
Why do I feel sad when I see those floating feathers?
The natural world is like a mirror for my mind.

Format and Examples

After students have assembled three or four scrapbook journal pages, they can begin to inter-leaf writing pages with them. Again, you may wish to supply a model. The words you or students write may have a direct relationship to scrapbook items, or relate to other experiences of that day.

Poets move from impressions and sensations to words. As students build their scrapbook journal pages, they can begin to add to them phrases and sentences that represent the three special characteristics of poetry: imagery, feeling, and insight.

Imagery Words, phrases, or sentences that are interesting in themselves because of the way they sound or because of the mental pictures they conjure up. Examples:

◆ I heard someone say <u>blue</u> <u>poodle</u>.

◆ I saw <u>floating</u> <u>feathers</u> on a silent pond.

◆ My dad said, "I need a dollar," but I thought he said, "I need a collar."

Feelings Statements or questions based on emotional reactions to what was sensed. Examples:

◆ I felt angry that someone would dye a poodle blue.

◆ Why do I feel sad when I see those floating feathers?

◆ I felt giggly picturing my dad with a collar.

Insights Ideas or beliefs that pop into mind. Examples:

◆ Pets have to put up with a lot of nonsense from their owners.

◆ The natural world is like a mirror for my mind.

◆ You have to listen closely to hear the message.

Moving into Poems

Most students will soon realize that the images, feelings, and insights they've noted in their scrapbook journals are the stuff of which poems are made. To affirm their discovery, use the modeling strategy to show how to juggle and play with, add to and subtract from, written phrases and sentences to create a poem. Example:

> **Floating feathers, silent pond...**
> **Why am I sad to see them?**
> **Maybe I am sad already,**
> **And the pond is my mirror.**

Suggest that students work with partners or independently to write poems that emanate from journal notes. Encourage students to share their poems with the class. Ask the audience to comment on images, feelings, and ideas they especially like.

Going On

Review with the class how their scrapbook journals helped them develop ideas for poems. Discuss ways they can continue to use their journals. You'll find other suggestions in Project 2, pages 44–49.

Start-up Ideas and Tips

Invite students to think about poetry by sharing the following poem, and then try some of the activities.

Give Me a Poem

Give me a poem as soft as sleep;
as dangerous as money;
as bitter as a nasty pill;
as sweet as summer honey;
and wrap it in a web of words,
as strong and fine as silk
as free as flocks of wheeling birds
as nourishing as milk.

If you give me a poem like that, I'll tell you what I'll do—
If you give me a poem like that, I'll give one back to you!

—*Helen H. Moore*

> **TEACHER TIP**
>
> Make poetry a part of your classroom environment. Select favorite poems, rhymed and unrhymed, to read aloud in spare moments during the day. Encourage students to select and read favorite poems, too.

Read the poem through a second time, then ask students to identify the different ways the poet describes a poem. List each way on the board and have students tell what the poet promises to do at the end of the poem. Ask students to meet the poet's challenge by making up poems of their own that fulfill her criteria. Share and discuss students' poetic responses.

Poetry Is Personal

Distribute copies of the poetry inventory on the next page and allow time for students to complete it. Then have them discuss their responses in small groups. Follow with a whole-class discussion in which students give general reactions to poetry. Encourage them to tell how they feel about hearing, reading, writing, and reciting poetry, and to name favorite poets or poems.

> **TEACHER TIP**
>
> Before assigning poetry writing pages, you may want to have students play the warm-up game on page 19.

Penny Poems

Obtain a shiny penny for each student in your class. Laminate each penny onto a piece of tagboard with the phrase *A Penny for Your Thoughts* on it. Begin your poetry unit by asking students to think about the future—a wish they hope for, or a dream they have. Ask them to write a poem about this thought. Give each student one of the pennies to spark ideas and to keep as a reminder of the poem. You can collect the "penny poems" in a class folder or display them on a class bulletin board.

Poetry Packs

One way to help students find topics for lively and meaningful poems is to have them write about things of value to them. Invite them to make "poetry packs." Have each student bring in a shoe box or lock-top plastic bag that holds an assortment of treasured souvenirs or keepsakes. Students can use this poetry pack to stimulate freewriting of images or phrases, which can later grow into complete poems.

Name _____

Focus on Poetry

Some people say that poems are feelings or experiences set to words. What comes to mind when you think about poetry? Write a response to each question below to help you clarify your ideas.

1. Are poems harder to understand than stories? Why? _____

_____

_____

2. Arc the best poems the ones that are funny or silly? What other kinds of poems can you think of? _____

_____

_____

_____

3. Should poetry always rhyme? _____

_____

_____

4. Why is reading poems aloud a good way to appreciate them?

_____

_____

_____

5. Can poems be about anything? List some things you might like to write poems about. _____

_____

_____

_____

More To Try! ➤ **What does this statement mean to you?** *Poetry needs fresh language. Write your response on the back of this page.*

Family Letter

Your classroom poets will be eager to share their work with those at home. Try these activities to acquaint everyone with your poetry plans.

◆ Reproduce and send home the letter on this page to explain how you will use poetry in the classroom and how those at home can help.

◆ Make available a list of poetry books (see page 72) that families might consult for poetry enjoyment at home. If possible, you might consider sending home poetry anthologies on a rotating basis.

◆ Send home the reproducible on the next page so that students can share this activity with their families.

◆ Be sure to invite families to your Poetry Tea (see page 20). Place a sign-up sheet near the door so you can record your guests' names. Then follow up by mailing out thank-you postcards to visitors to let them know how much their presence meant.

Dear Parent or Caregiver,

Our class is focusing on poetry right now, and we'd like to share some thoughts about it with you.

Poetry is a wonderful way of exploring language. It enables students to express thoughts, feelings, and observations about their environment in thousands of different ways. It is a means of connecting with other imaginations.

You can help develop your child's appreciation of poetry and language in the following ways:

1. Include poetry in the reading that you do together. There are many delightful books of poetry for young people available in libraries and bookstores.

2. Encourage your son or daughter to share original poems with you. Your interest and positive response will mean a lot.

3. If you've ever memorized any poems, recite them for your child. Choose a short verse to memorize and say it aloud together.

4. Enjoy the poetry that you and your child share!

Sincerely,

Name _____

A Silly Side-by-Side Poem

Share this poem and poetry activity with someone at home.

The Folks Who Live In Backwards Town

The folks who live in backwards town
Are inside out and upside down.
They wear their hats inside their heads
And go to sleep beneath their beds.
They only eat apple peeling
And take their walks across the ceiling.

—*Mary Ann Hoberman*

Imagine you're a visitor to Backwards Town. Use Mary Ann Hoberman's poem as a springboard to write more kooky verses about the mixed-up folks who live there. (The first one is done for you.) Then, ask family members to contribute verses. When you're finished, read the new poem aloud. And don't forget to share it with your classmates tomorrow…or is that *yesterday?*

"The Folks Who Live in Backwards Town" from *Hello and Goodbye* by Mary Ann Hoberman. Copyright © renewed 1987 Mary Ann Hoberman. Reprinted by permission of Gina Macoby Literary Agency.

They *mess up their hair before heading to school.*
And *wear their pajamas into the town pool.*

They _____
And _____

They _____
And _____

They _____
And _____

They _____
And _____

 **More To Try!**   Draw a humorous illustration to go with your poem.

Poetry Pockets

Encourage students to discover and share poetry with this interactive bulletin board.

TEACHER TIP

You'll find poems on pages 12, 15, 20, 22, 23, 25, 29, 30, 33, 34, 39, 40, 42, 43, 47, 48, 53, 56, 57, 58, 59, 60, 61, 63, 65, 67.

Materials: craft paper ◆ stapler ◆ pocket patterns (next page) ◆ scissors ◆ paste ◆ tagboard ◆ markers, fabric scraps, and other materials for decorating pockets ◆ selected poems

Steps:

1. Cover a bulletin board with craft paper.

2. Make enough copies of the pocket pattern so that you have 13 pockets. Use them to write out the title "Poetry Pockets." Affix them to the display.

3. Enlarge and reproduce more copies of the patterns, making several copies of each. Paste the pocket shapes to tagboard and cut around each pattern.

4. Invite students to decorate the pockets using fabric scraps, markers, and other materials.

5. Staple the pockets to the bulletin board along the bottom and both sides. Leave the top of each pocket open.

6. On the outside of each pocket, write a category, such as animals, places, people, tongue twisters, colors, food, favorite things, nonsense.

7. Place a poem in each pocket (add an element of surprise by folding it). Invite students to visit the display to pick a pocket of poems. Encourage them to add favorite poems to the pockets, both their own and poems they discover in classroom resources.

Reproduce the pocket shapes on this page and use them to write out the title "Poetry Pockets." Enlarge the pocket shapes to hold poems when stapled to the board. (See directions on page 16.) Invite students to decorate the pockets using markers, fabric scraps, and other available materials before stapling them to the bulletin board display.

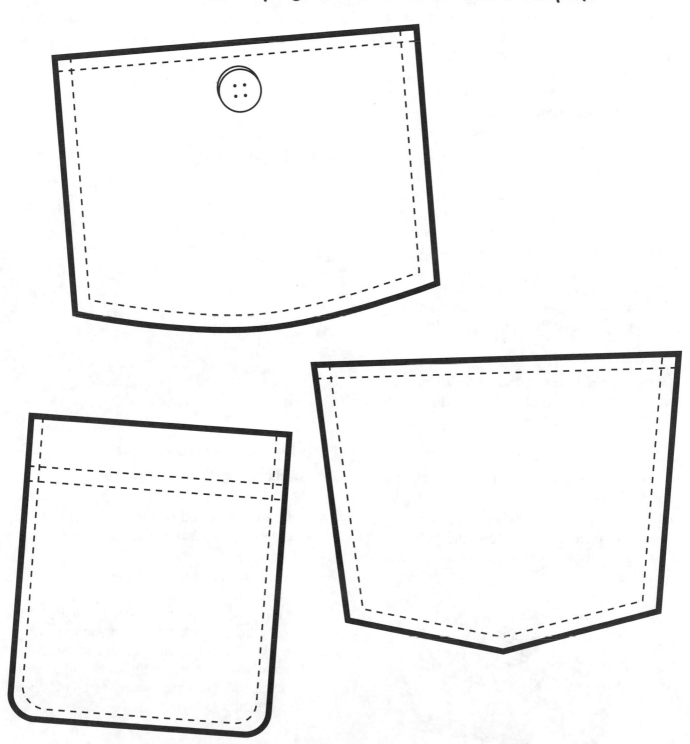

More Powerful Poetry Starters

Poetry Without Pressure

Poetry is a powerful tool for promoting language development in children. As Judith Steinbergh explains in *Reading and Writing Poetry: A Guide for Teachers* (Scholastic Professional Books, 1994): "It pushes children to think about feeling and meaning, to reach for symbol and metaphor, and to articulate abstract ideas. It guides children to listen to language and choose words and phrasing with care."

But the constraints of an ordinary school day may not be conducive to the time a poet needs to play with and develop ideas for poetry. To ease the pressure some children feel about writing poetry in class, allow time to generate and explore ideas, write, read aloud, share, revise, and publish. Encourage students to revisit their poems after a couple of days before making final revisions. (See also the tips on page 36.)

Grab Bag Poetry

How many times have you heard "What can I write about?" With these poetry starters, an idea is just a grab bag away.

Grab Bag 1: Place Poems

◆ Put pictures of places cut from magazines in a bag or box.

◆ Write out directions that ask students to choose a picture, list as many things as they can about that place, then use that list to write a place poem.

Grab Bag 2: "If" Poems

◆ Write names for people, places, animals, colors, things, musical instruments, foods, and so on, on slips of paper. Place in a box or bag.

◆ Have children randomly select a paper and write a poem that starts "If I were a(n) _____."

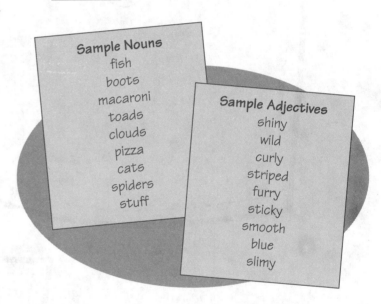

Sample Nouns
fish
boots
macaroni
toads
clouds
pizza
cats
spiders
stuff

Sample Adjectives
shiny
wild
curly
striped
furry
sticky
smooth
blue
slimy

Grab Bag 3: Parts of Speech Poems

◆ Label one bag *Nouns*. Label another *Adjectives*.

◆ Write adjectives and nouns on strips of paper, one per strip (see samples). Place in corresponding bags.

◆ Demonstrate by randomly selecting one adjective and one noun from the bags. Put them together to make your title (for example, "Blue Pizza"). Invite students to help you write a poem about this silly subject. Encourage students to add their own nouns and adjectives to the bags, too. (You may want to sign off on their contributions first.)

Name _____

Writing Warm-Ups

Joggers do stretching exercises to get their muscles in shape before they run. This game will help you flex your "writing muscles" before starting on a poem.

Materials: this page ◆ a penny ◆ a pencil ◆ scrap paper
◆ clock or watch with a second hand (optional)

Directions:

1. Choose a partner.

2. Take turns tossing a penny. Tails, you move **1** space. Heads, you move **2** spaces.

3. When you land on a space, challenge yourself to *creatively* fulfill the mini-assignment in thirty seconds or less. Do the writing warm-up on a piece of scrap paper. Then share it with your partner. It can be funny or factual—anything goes!

4. The first player to reach "Poet's Corner" is the winner.

5. After you're all warmed up, take your time and write a really cool poem.

START HERE

Find three adjectives to describe POPCORN

Use these two words in a rhyme: **Square/Hair**

Complete this sentence: **Rain sounds like...**

Use these two words in a rhyme: **Freeze/Breeze**

Complete this sentence: **Spring smells like...**

Find three adjectives to describe a

Use these two words in a rhyme: **House/Mouse**

Find three adjectives to describe a

Use these two words in a rhyme: **Hill/Spill**

Complete this sentence: **Red is a...**

Complete this sentence: **Cotton candy tastes like...**

POET'S CORNER You win!

Complete this sentence: **Blue is a...**

Find three adjectives to describe a

Use these two words in a rhyme: **Clown/Town**

WRAP-UP ACTIVITY

Poetry Tea

As a culminating activity, invite students to plan a poetry tea, complete with poetry readings, refreshments, and guests.

Here are some suggestions for planning an event that will allow students to showcase their talents in different ways. Because not all students may feel comfortable sharing poetry aloud, you'll find ideas here for ways to involve everyone.

Interactive Invitations

Have students fold paper to create invitations. Brainstorm information about the event and post a master at the Poetry Center (see page 52). Have children copy this information on invitations they create. In addition to What, Where, When, include a line that says: "Please bring something that is yellow." Have students copy favorite poems on the covers (their own or someone else's). Finally, invite guests to bring a favorite poem to share if they wish.

Preparation

Offer several ways for students to share poems at the tea. Students might create displays, read aloud favorite poems, prepare musical or dramatic interpretations, or help design poetic party favors—poems written and illustrated on special paper and rolled up and tied with colorful ribbon or string. Pull together a tea service: A fancy milk pitcher, sugar bowl, and teapots will add atmosphere to the event. Plan to serve herb teas and the cookies from the poem on page 63.

A Collaborative Poem

Plan to have a student read aloud the poem "Yellow" by David McCord. Then ask guests to share whatever they brought that is yellow. Add to the list by inviting everyone to name other things that are yellow. *(Yellow is a lemon drop, a bug light, a flower.)* Put everyone's ideas together to create a poem about the color yellow.

Yellow

Green is go,
and red is stop,
and yellow is peaches
with cream on top.

Earth is brown,
and blue is sky;
yellow looks well
on a butterfly.

Clouds are white,
black, pink, or mocha;
yellow's a dish of
tapioca.

—*David McCord*

TEACHER TIP

Make large poetry pads available so that groups of students and guests can develop poems together.

Skills-Practice Mini-Lessons...

...to use as your young poets need them

Exploring the World of Lewis Carroll

Invite students to read "The Walrus and the Carpenter." Then explain that it is one of many nonsense poems found in Lewis Carroll's two most famous children's books—*Alice's Adventures in Wonderland* and its sequel, *Through the Looking-Glass.*

Responses to Reading

Give each student a copy of the poem on the next two pages. Then read aloud the first few stanzas. What clues can students find that this is probably a nonsense poem? As students read their copies of the poem independently, suggest that they record their reactions and questions in a journal. Encourage them to note any words, such as billows or beseech, whose meanings they might want to check in a dictionary. Once students have read the poem, bring the class together to share their notes. At what point did students realize what the walrus and carpenter had in mind? Did either of the characters seem to feel remorse about the oysters' fate?

Looking at Lewis Carroll

Students may be interested to learn that Lewis Carroll was the pseudonym or pen name for Charles L. Dodgson, who also wrote books on logic and mathematics and had a fine reputation as a children's photographer. As a boy, Carroll was full of ingenious ideas and was constantly inventing puzzles and writing nonsense rhymes. As Lewis Carroll, he had many young friends with whom he corresponded; one girl named Alice Liddell, was Alice's namesake. Invite students to write their own reactions to the poem as a letter addressed to Carroll. Do they have a favorite stanza or image in the poem? Why do they like it?

TEACHER TIP
You'll find more about nonsense poems on page 55.

Jabberwocky

Carroll's famous nonsense poem, "Jabberwocky," is found in the opening chapter of *Through the Looking-Glass.* Share the first stanza of "Jabberwocky" with students and invite them to make up their own glossary of meanings for the nonsense words.

from *Jabberwocky*

Twas brillig, and the slithy toves
    Did gyre and gimble in the wabe:
All mimsy were the borogoves,
    And the mome raths outgrabe.

Doublets

Lewis Carroll delighted in wordplay. He created many acrostic and double-crostic puzzles for publication and also came up with a new form of word puzzle called "doublets," in which one word is transformed into another by changing one letter at a time. For example HEAD can be transformed into TAIL as shown at right.

```
HEAD
heal
teal
tell
tall
TAIL
```

Challenge students to puzzle through the following Doublets. The words in upper-case letters are transformed.

Change WET to DRY.
Make HARE into SOUP.
PITCH TENTS.

Change OAT to RYE.
Get WOOD from TREE.
Prove GRASS to be GREEN.

Name_____

LITERATURE LINK

The Walrus and the Carpenter

This famous nonsense poem is recited by twins named Tweedledum and Tweedledee in a book called *Through the Looking Glass*. It is by Lewis Carroll, the author of *Alice's Adventures in Wonderland*.

As you read this humorous rhyme, jot down your reactions in your poetry journal. This might include your response to the characters, the images in the poem, or the events Carroll describes.

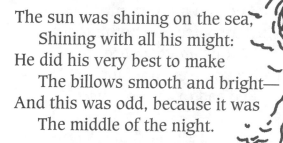

The sun was shining on the sea,
    Shining with all his might:
He did his very best to make
    The billows smooth and bright—
And this was odd, because it was
    The middle of the night.

The moon was shining sulkily,
    Because she thought the sun
Had got no business to be there
    After the day was done—
"It's very rude of him," she said,
    "To come and spoil the fun!"

The sea was wet as wet could be,
    The sands were dry as dry.
You could not see a cloud, because
    No cloud was in the sky:
No birds were flying overhead—
    There were no birds to fly.

The Walrus and the Carpenter
    Were walking close at hand:
They wept like anything to see
    Such quantities of sand:
"If this were only cleared away,"
    They said, "it would be grand!"

"If seven maids with seven mops
    Swept it for half a year,
Do you suppose," the Walrus said,
    "That they could get it clear?"
"I doubt it," said the Carpenter,
    And shed a bitter tear.

"O, Oysters, come and walk with us!"
    The Walrus did beseech.
"A pleasant talk, a pleasant walk,
    Along the briny beach:
We cannot do with more than four,
    To give a hand to each."

The eldest Oyster looked at him,
    But never a word he said;
The eldest Oyster winked his eye,
    And shook his heavy head—
Meaning to say he did not choose
    To leave the oyster bed.

But four young Oysters hurried up,
    All eager for the treat:
Their coats were brushed, their faces washed,
    Their shoes were clean and neat—
And this was odd, because, you know,
    They hadn't any feet.

23

Name_____

Four other Oysters followed them,
   And yet another four;
And thick and fast they came at last,
   And more, and more, and more—
All hopping through the frothy waves,
   And scrambling to the shore.

The Walrus and the Carpenter
   Walked on a mile or so,
And then they rested on a rock
   Conveniently low:
And all the little Oysters stood
   And waited in a row.

"The time has come," the Walrus said,
   "To talk of many things:
Of shoes—and ships—and sealing wax—
   Of cabbages—and kings—
And why the sea is boiling hot—
   And whether pigs have wings."

"But wait a bit," the Oysters cried,
   "Before we have our chat;
For some of us are out of breath,
   And all of us are fat!"
"No hurry!" said the Carpenter.
   They thanked him much for that.

"A loaf of bread," the Walrus said,
   "Is what we chiefly need:
Pepper and vinegar besides
   Are very good indeed—
Now, if you're ready, Oysters dear,
   We can begin to feed."

"But not on us!" the Oysters cried,
   Turning a little blue.
"After such kindness, that would be
   A dismal thing to do!"
"The night is fine," the Walrus said.
   "Do you admire the view?"

"It was so kind of you to come!
   And you are very nice!"
The Carpenter said nothing but
   "Cut us another slice.
I wish you were not quite so deaf—
   I've had to ask you twice!"

"It seems a shame," the Walrus said,
   "To play them such a trick,
After we've brought them out so far,
   And made them trot so quick!"
The Carpenter said nothing but
   "The butter's spread too thick!"

"I weep for you," the Walrus said:
   "I deeply sympathize."
With sobs and tears he sorted out
   Those of the largest size,
Holding his pocket handkerchief
   Before his streaming eyes.

"O Oysters," said the Carpenter,
   "You've had a pleasant run!
Shall we be trotting home again?"
   But answer came there none—
And this was scarcely odd, because
   They'd eaten every one.

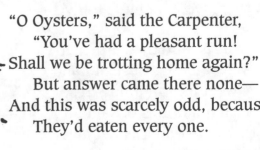

—*Lewis Carroll*

Similes and Metaphors

Similes and metaphors are often-used figures of speech in poetry. With these activities, students will learn how to recognize and write them. Start with similes.

What Is a Simile?

Before students actively participate in this exercise, introduce or reinforce that a simile is a comparison between two things using the words *like* or *as.* For example, "My eyes are *like* two meatballs sitting on white plates, and my feet are *as* long *as* two boats sailing on a green tiled sea."

Next read the poem at right, explaining that the author, a Native American Navajo, uses similes to describe his horse. Ask students to listen carefully to the pictures the similes create in their minds, because in a little while they will be asked to write similes describing themselves.

Making Connections

1. Read the poem again and ask students to raise their hands each time they hear a simile.

2. Invite students to paint pictures of the horse described in the poem. Copy the poem onto a poster pad so they can refer to it as they work.

> ### TEACHER TIP
> Explain to the class the meaning of *agate* and *fetlock* ahead of time, so they aren't confused during the actual reading.

The War God's Horse Song

I am the Turquoise Woman's Son

On top of Belted Mountain beautiful horses
slim like a weasel

My horse has a hoof like striped agate
his fetlock is like fine eagle plume
his legs are like quick lightning

My horse's body is like an eagle-feathered arrow

My horse has a tail like a trailing black cloud.

I put flexible goods on my horse's back

The Holy Wind blows through his mane
his mane is made of rainbows

My horse's ears are made of round corn

My horse's eyes are made of stars

My horse's head is made of mixed waters
    (from the holy waters)
    (he never knows thirst)

My horse's teeth are made of white shell

The long rainbow is in his mouth for a bridle

with it I guide him

When my horse neighs
different-colored horses follow

When my horse neighs
different-colored sheep follow

I am wealthy from my horse

Before me peaceful
Behind me peaceful
Under me peaceful
Over me peaceful
Peaceful voice when he neighs
I am everlasting and peaceful
I stand for my horse

—*Navajo; adapted from Dane and Mary Roberts Coolidge*

Using Similes to Write Self-Portraits

TEACHER TIP
Encourage students to find more similes in other poems. A good place to start is "Give Me a Poem on page 12.

Begin by modeling the thinking process that you want students to follow when they write their "Self-Portraits." (See page 28, but don't give copies of the reproducible to students yet.) First ask students to touch their hair. Next pose a question: "What does your hair feel like?" Possible answers might include:

"My hair feels like dry summer grass."

"My hair feels like porcupine quills."

"My hair feels like tangled thread."

Explain to students that besides the texture of their hair, they might consider its color and shape. For instance, someone with long flowing hair might say: "My hair looks like a waterfall flowing down rocky mountain shoulders." Someone with blond hair might say: "My hair looks like streaks of sunlight coming through a window."

Put the following simile reminder list on the board.

Explain that the rows of dots inserted after "like" are to remind students to add plenty of their own details, and not just one or two words to complete their similes. Have students practice writing similes about their hair. As students share their similes, ask classmates to identify the two things being compared.

COLOR like............

LOOKS like............
(shape)

FEELS like............
(texture)

What Is a Metaphor?

Explain that a metaphor is similar to a simile since it also compares two things. What makes a metaphor different is that it is a more powerful assertion of the comparison and doesn't include like or as.

For example, removing the word like in the following simile transforms it into the stronger comparison of a metaphor.

"My hair is like a swirling black cloud"
becomes
"My hair is a swirling black cloud."

Brainstorming

Before passing out the reproducible on the next page, brainstorm areas of the body you want students to concentrate on in their writing. For example, if you are studying the skeletal system, you might want to make a list of solely skeletal parts, or if you are studying internal organs, you might want your list to include kidneys, heart, and lungs and their respective functions.

Or you might also want to telescope your class's explorations to include only the parts of a hand (nails, metatarsals, knuckles) or the circulatory system (plasma, corpuscles, veins, arteries).

TEACHER TIP

This is a great opportunity to introduce or reinforce subject-verb agreement by stressing how the verbs *is* and *are* must agree with either a singular or plural subject.

Ending the Poem

Point out the ending in the reproducible self-portrait poem on the next page. This offers students another opportunity to use their imaginations in an enjoyable way. Brainstorm some of the places students might choose to live and eat. For example, "I live in a computer and eat wires/gears/disks/memory" or "I live in a shoe and eat wig-

gly toes," or "I live in a rain forest and eat…" To make their endings more interesting, announce that no one is allowed to live in a house and eat food.

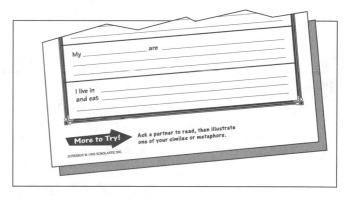

Family "Portraits"

As a variation, suggest that students choose a family member and describe the person's qualities using similes and metaphors. Encourage a wide range of choices for this exercise, ranging from "Little Brother" or "Mom Portraits" to a portrait of a family pet.

Name_____

Metaphors, Similes, and Me

You can create a self-portrait with words. Use this chart as a guide to write similes and metaphors about yourself. Use lots of interesting details and add more spaces if you need them. It's okay to cross out or add words to make each simile and metaphor your own special creation. Have fun! When you're done, you'll have a poem about you!

My _____ is like _____
_____
_____

My _____ are like _____
_____
_____

My _____ is a _____
_____
_____

My _____ are _____
_____
_____

I live in _____
and eat _____
_____

 **More To Try!** Ask a partner to read one of your similes or metaphors and then illustrate it.

28

SKILLS-PRACTICE MINI-LESSON / PERSONIFICATION

Who's Who in a Poem

In some poems, things or even seasons take on a human personality. As you read aloud this poem, ask the class to visualize Winter. How is this season dressed? What accessories does Winter wear?

Packing Up

Winter,
Put your things away!
Into your storebox
Let there go
The myriad flakes of whirling snow.
Pack up the winds
That sway the trees
And fold them neatly.
Over there,
Pile the layers
Of ice and frost.
One by one, stack on stack,
Put the crystal icicles back—
Let none be lost!
When all are in, shut the box,
And turn the key, and snap the locks.
Then, leave a note for all to read:
WINTER HAS GONE TO SPRING AND SEED

—*Grace Cornell Tall*

Wordplay

Point out that the poet has fun playing with words in this poem. Reread Winter's note and ask students to think about the meaning of the idiomatic phrase "to go to seed." What double meaning does this phrase have in the context of this poem?

"Packing Up" by Grace Cornell Tall. First appeared in *Cricket, the Magazine for Children,* March 1994. Reprinted by permission of the author.

Act It Out!

This poem presents great dramatic possibilities. Have students make cutouts of Winter's "accessories" mentioned in the poem. Then, as you recite the poem aloud, neatly pack Winter's garb away in an old suitcase or backpack. They might end with a flourish by taping Winter's farewell note on top of the luggage!

Seasonal Garb

Ask the class to imagine a similar description for the other seasons. What would each season pack away when it's time to depart? Alternatively, what would the seasons take out of their trunks right after their arrival? Use "Packing Up" as a model and have students write their own poems in which a season or some other natural phenomenon has a personality. You may want to explain that this is called personification.

SKILLS-PRACTICE MINI-LESSON / ONOMATOPOEIA

Jingling, Tinkling Bells

Children's everyday lives are filled with sounds—and words that imitate those sounds. You can use their own language to introduce onomatopoeia. Children will quickly grasp the technique and will soon use it in their own poetry to create sensory-rich images.

You might introduce onomatopoeia by sharing a student's poem that employs this device. Follow up with this excerpt from "The Bells" by Edgar Allan Poe. Ask students to listen for words that help create bell-like effects.

from *The Bells*

Hear the sledges with the bells—
    Silver bells!
What a world of merriment their melody foretells!
    How they tinkle, tinkle, tinkle,
        In the icy air of night!
    While the stars that oversprinkle
    All the heavens seem to twinkle
    With a crystalline delight;
    Keeping time, time, time,
    In a sort of Runic rhyme,
To the tintinnabulation that so musically wells
    From the bells, bells, bells, bells,
        Bells, bells, bells—
From the jingling and the tinkling of the bells.

—*Edgar Allan Poe*

> **TEACHER TIP**
>
> Help students look for examples of other poetic devices in "The Bells," such as alliteration and assonance.

Musical Words

Ask students to name words in "The Bells" that sound like their meaning. *Twinkle, tintinnabulation, jingling* are a few. If possible, pass out copies of the entire poem and have students work in pairs or small groups to find more. You might ask students to underline or highlight the words they find. Add these words to the chart created in the Sounds Like activity below and post for easy reference.

Sounds Like

Play a game of sound association. Prepare a list of words that children may associate sounds with, such as *mosquito*. Let students take turns suggesting words they think of when they hear mosquito (such as *buzz* and *whack*). After a few rounds, let students try giving the starter word. Record the sound words on a chart and display at the poetry center. (See page 8.)

Rhyme-Around

Here's a poetry game for pairs, small groups, or for the whole class.

Object: To make rhymes for the key word. The first team to get 5 points wins.

Materials: 15 index cards, with the following key words on them:

day   skate   less   sky   nine   phone
far   key   deep   bill   show
flew   sure   hug   mom

Rules:
1. Divide the class or group into two teams. Each team picks a secretary to write down the rhymes his or her teammates say. Shuffle the cards.

2. Decide which team goes first and the order of players on each team. The lead-off player picks a key word card at random and reads it aloud. This player says a word that rhymes with that word. The secretary records the word.

3. Play shifts to the other team. The first player from that team says another rhyme for the key word. The secretary records it. Play shifts back to the first team. Now the second player tries to make a different rhyme for the same key word. Play alternates between teams and down the line-up of players.

4. If a player cannot think of a rhyming word, the round ends, and the other team gets 1 point. The next player on the other team picks a new key word card and play continues in the same way.

5. If someone repeats a word, that player gets one chance to come up with another rhyme. If the second-chance word has also been said before, the other team gets 1 point. A new key word is chosen and play continues in the same way.

You can vary this game in many ways:
◆ Start with different key words.
◆ Allow rhyming words of any number of syllables, as long as the final syllable rhymes with the key word.
◆ Let teams brainstorm for one minute to list words that rhyme with the key word. Whichever team has more rhyming words when time is called earns 1 point. The first team to earn 5 points wins.
◆ Make a "rhyme chain" with the whole class. One student picks the key word card, then play moves around the room as each student gets to say a rhyming word. When the chain "breaks," that student picks the next key word.

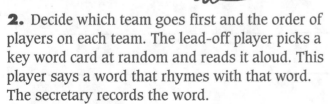

Name_____

Hink Pink,
What Do You Think?

Here's a rhyme-time challenge to try with a partner.

A *hink pink* is a pair of one-syllable words that rhyme. *Hink pink* **is** a hink pink. So are *brain drain*, *June tune*, and *fat cat*.

The *clue shoe* contains some hink pinks. Match each hink pink with its clue. Here's an example: A cozy place to read is a *book nook*.

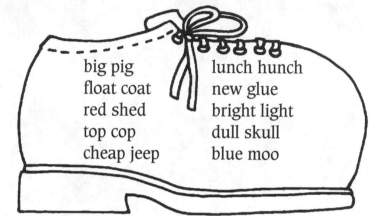

big pig   lunch hunch
float coat   new glue
red shed   bright light
top cop   dull skull
cheap jeep   blue moo

1. Large hog _____

2. Fresh paste _____

3. Strong lamp _____

4. Small scarlet hut _____

5. Inexpensive vehicle _____

6. Boring skeleton part_____

7. Guess about a midday meal _____

8. Most important police officer _____

9. Sound an unhappy cow makes _____

10. Warm garment a sailor might wear _____

More To Try!

A *hinky pinky* is like a hink pink, but each word in the pair has two syllables. *Older folder, silly Millie, phony pony* are hinky pinkies. Make up some hinky pinkies and clues for them. Give them to a classmate to solve. If you want a BIG challenge, try a *hinkety pinkety*! Can you figure out what it is?

32

LITERATURE LINK

Humor with Homonyms

Words are the tools of a poet, and many poets use words in clever ways. Introduce students to this idea with the poem on this page.

Review the meaning of homonyms: words with the same pronunciation and often the same spelling, but with different meanings. Examples include *key* (for a lock or for a musical piece), *boot* (footwear or how to start a computer), and *low* (not high or the sound a cow makes). Share the poem "Have You Ever Seen?" with the class. At first reading, put on a serious tone and a straight face, but alert students to listen for homonyms.

Have You Ever Seen?

Have you ever seen a sheet on a river bed?
Or a single hair from a hammer's head?
Has the foot of a mountain any toes?
And is there a pair of garden hose?
Does the needle ever wink its eye?
Why doesn't the wing of a building fly?
Can you tickle the ribs of a parasol?
Or open the trunk of a tree at all?
Are the teeth of a rake ever going to bite?
Have the hands of a clock any left or right?
Can the garden plot be deep and dark?
And what is the sound of the birch's bark?

—*Anonymous*

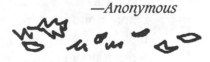

◆ Reread the poem and ask volunteers to identify each homonym. Discuss how the poet uses these words to create humor.

◆ Invite students to choose a line of the poem to illustrate. Display students' pictures and have the class guess which line is illustrated.

◆ Work with the class to make a list of other homonyms. Then suggest that students use these to write new verses for the poem.

TEACHER TIP
Provide some *Amelia Bedelia* books students can browse through for other examples of wordplay that might inspire them to write funny poems.

Ticklish Tips
Here are some helpful hints from poet Douglas Florian on writing funny poems.

◆ Use your imagination. Think of weird, wacky, impossible, silly, and outrageous things that could happen in a topsy-turvy world.

◆ Make rhymes by going through the alphabet. Start with a sound and try different beginnings for it: oodle, doodle, froodle, noodle…

◆ Use words that sound funny to you, such as doohickey, sproing, or gizmo. Make up silly words if they sound good to your ear.

◆ Exaggerate!

SKILLS-PRACTICE MINI-LESSON / COLOR IN POETRY

Poetry Paint Box

Many poems are filled with references to colors—both ordinary and exotic. Other poems seem to paint pictures in the mind's eye. Use the following poem to launch students into an exploration of color from the poet's point of view.

Before, During, and After the Poem

Before reading the poem, invite students to brainstorm a list of colors. In addition to the primary and secondary ones, challenge them to come up with as many unusual color names as they can recall from their jumbo crayon packs! Then, as you share the poem, ask them to listen for other exotic color names and how they are used. Have pairs of students try rereading the poem as a dialogue between two people, using different voices to signify each speaker. Point out how the quotation marks can help them figure out each part.

The Paint Box

"Cobalt and umber and ultramarine,
Ivory black and emerald green—
What shall I paint to give pleasure to you?"
"Paint for me somebody utterly new."

"I have painted you tigers in crimson and white."
"The colors were good and you painted aright."
"I have painted the cook and a camel in blue
And a panther in purple." "You painted them true.

"Now mix me a color that nobody knows,
And paint me a country where nobody goes.
And put in it people a little like you,
Watching a unicorn drinking the dew."

—*E. V. Rieu*

"The Paint Box" by E. V. Rieu, General Editor of the Penguin Classics. By permission of Dominic Rieu.

Poetry Palette

Choose a color of the day and celebrate it by reading a poem from Mary O'Neill's classic *Hailstones and Halibut Bones: Adventures in Color* (Doubleday, 1989) Inspired by the poems, students can create photomontages or collages with pictures, words, and phrases associated with the color of their choice.

Mix Me a Color

Have students recall the colors in the poem. If possible, have them find color swatches or crayons that are cobalt, umber, ultramarine, and crimson. Then, using paints, challenge them to create and name a new color and use it to paint a "country where nobody goes." Some students may want to go one step beyond and write a poem about this country or the color that they've mixed. Then use the poems and paintings to explore how writing a poem is similar to creating a picture of a place that exists only in the imagination.

Name_____

Meet Poet Bobbi Katz

Bobbi Katz worked for many years as a book editor. Now she writes poetry full time and her work appears in many anthologies. One of her favorite things to do (when she's not working on a poem) is to play the African drums. Here's what she said in an interview about her work as a poet.

What got you interested in poetry?

When I was growing up, we had very few books. But I did have some alphabet blocks, and could see that those letters were part of the world around me. Emmy, a woman who took care of me while my mother worked, would read poems to me from several books kept in a cupboard. We called that cupboard "the library." It was a treat to open the cupbaord and have the words of the poems come to life. I've loved words ever since. The words from "in the library" inspired one of my first poems, "Ammonia Begonia."

How do you get ideas for your poems?

There are a million more ideas than there are minutes in the day. We just have to open our eyes and ears and let them come in. I keep a journal. In it I write bits of poems, pre-poems, snippets of conversations, and images of anything that might fit into a poem later. I also have a bulletin board full of note cards, photos, and newspaper clippings—all inspirations and ideas for poems. For example, I wrote a poem, "A Kid Like Me," when I looked at pictures of my kids rolling in the grass.

Read Bobbi Katz's poem "What If" on the poster. The ten words Bobbi said she wouldn't want to be without are: *wind, daffodils whispering, pitter patter, rhythm, sky, surf, footprints, drimbeats,* and *silence.* What favorite words would you choose? Why?

_____

_____

_____

_____

_____

_____

Share your list with a partner.

Write a poem about your words. You might write an "if" poem: "If I were a word" or "If I were the word _____."

35

Name_____

Six Finishing-up Tips

Sometimes poet Bobbi Katz gets a poem just right the first time. But it can take as long as a couple of years. She often makes changes in tiny ways—changing a word or a line break. Her guide in making revisions? Less is more. Here, Katz shares tips for making revisions. Keep this copy with your poetry scrapbook.

1. Leave a lot of space between each line of poetry so that you have room to make changes and can see them.

2. Give yourself time to put all of your thoughts down first. Then begin editing. You might find you have several poems in this first attempt.

3. Think of a poem as a vitamin. It has to hold a lot of energy in a small container. As you read your poem aloud, look at each word. Can some be stronger? More specific?

4. If you aren't writing in rhyme, try other ways to make your poem hang together. Repetition is a big help in creating rhythm. That's when a poet uses a word or combination of words to begin or end each line or group of lines.

5. Try different ways of breaking each line. When you read your poem aloud, do the line breaks bring out certain words? Do they create pauses where you want them?

6. Take a break from your poem for a couple of days. (It helps to have a little distance.) Then go back to your poem and take a fresh look. Read it aloud again. Does it feel finished?

Here is one of the many drafts Bobbi Katz made for her poem "What If." Be sure to compare this draft to the final version on the poster.

I was working on this report about the environment

Endangered

When you think about the environment

I was writing about endangered species

Do you ever wonder "what if"?

Like what if there was a shortage of words?

What if words were suddenly endangered

Would people panic, hurrying to say things

just to get them said

or would they hoard their thoughts like misers,

afraid to use up their limited supply?

What if there was word pollution

and you couldn't use words safely the way you can't eat clams

from certain clam beds

or drink water? /from certain streams

Ten years ago, there were 20,00 elephants in Africa.

Now there are only 500 hundred elephants

What if there only five hundred words left?

Which fifty, which twenty, which ten words

would you save?

Which would you recycle, respect, repeat, replay,

write or say?

Our class is

We were doing reports about the environment

I was do

When I

spell out 500? other #'s?

Two Poetry Projects

1—Appreciating Poetry

2—Writing Poetry

Appreciating Poetry

For this five-assignment project, students will practice ways of responding to poetry, then explore ways poems evoke these responses.

GETTING STARTED
Make a Meaning Cluster

> "The reader who is illuminated is, in a real sense, the poem."
>
> —*H. M. Tomlinson*

In other words, a poem has the power to evoke a unique response from each reader. Students will feel comfortable with poetry if they learn the value of their personal response to each poem they read.

A good way to move into the multiple, personal meanings of a poem is to let students discover the multiple, personal meanings of a single word or phrase. With the class, brainstorm a meaning cluster around a word that has a lot of powerful connotations, as in the example at right.

Then have students work in groups of six, with three partner teams in each group. Assign each group a powerful word or phrase, such as *storm, school, a city street, night,* or *ocean.* Instruct partners to create meaning clusters, then share and compare the results with other pairs in their group. Bring the class together to discuss what these words mean to different people. Reinforce students' ideas by stressing the validity of each response in the clusters.

Talking About the Task
Input and Output

Recall the different clusters that students generated, then point out that each person brings something different—an experience, feeling, reaction—to a poem. This may temper the meaning or experience that the poet intended, so one reader's response may differ somewhat from another's. Use the following diagram to clarify this explanation.

FIRST ASSIGNMENT
Finding Meaning

lovely thoughts

hopes

DREAMS

plans

wishes

fantasies

On the chalkboard, build a meaning cluster with "Dreams" in the center. Add students' ideas and associations to the cluster. Then copy the following poem on the chalkboard and read it with the class.

Dreams

Hold fast to dreams
For if dreams die
Life is a broken-winged bird
That cannot fly.

Hold fast to dreams
For when dreams go
Life is a barren field
Frozen with snow.

—*Langston Hughes*

"Dreams" from *The Dream Keeper and Other Poems* by Langston Hughes. Copyright © 1932 by Alfred A. Knopf, Inc. Copyright renewed 1960 by Langston Hughes. Reprinted by permission of Alfred A. Knopf, Inc.

Discuss the poem with the class using prompt questions like these:

◆ What kind of dreams is the poet telling about?

◆ What do you think of when you imagine a "broken-winged bird"? A "field frozen with snow"?

◆ What do you think "barren" means? How can you find out if you are right?

◆ How can a dream "die"?

◆ What big idea is the poet writing about in this poem?

Then invite students to share their responses. Ask them what dreams they have that they want to "hold fast" to? How does this poem make them feel? What do they think about its message? Have students reread the poem, then discuss how discovering the meanings in the poem adds to their pleasure when they hear it again. At this point, students might want to add other ideas to their dream clusters.

SECOND ASSIGNMENT
Feelings About a Field

Readers come away from good poetry with strong feelings as well as with new insights. After exploring their emotional reactions to a poem, students can move on to explore (on the next page) some poetic strategies that elicit both ideas and feelings.

Write the title "The Old Field" on the chalkboard. Ask volunteers to call out instant associations to these words. Then read aloud the poem.

The Old Field

The old field is sad
Now the children have gone home.
They have played with him all afternoon,
Kicking the ball to him, and him
Kicking it back.

But now it is growing cold and dark.
He thinks of their warm breath, and their
Feet like little hot-water bottles.
A bit rough, some of them, but still...

And now, he thinks, there's not even a dog
To tickle me.
The gates are locked.
The birds don't like this nasty sneaking wind,
And nor does he.

—D. J. Enright

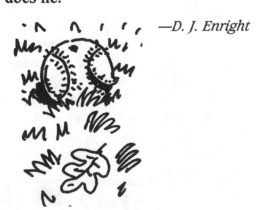

"The Old Field" from *Rhyme Time Rhyme* by D. J. Enright. Published by Chatto & Windus. Reprinted by permission of Watson, Little Ltd. as the licensing agents.

Responding to the Poem

In a quick round-robin, have students sum up with a word or two the feelings they have after hearing the poem. Write their responses on the chalkboard. (Examples: *sad, tired, curious, puzzled, frightened, sympathetic*) How do these feelings compare to those students mentioned before hearing the poem?

Use question prompts to encourage students to talk about the ideas in the poem.

◆ What's unusual about the field in this poem? *(The field is presented as if it were alive, thinking, and feeling, just like a human being.)*

◆ What time of day is it? What words and phrases tell you so?

◆ How does the field feel about the children? How does the field feel when they leave? How do you know?

Conclude by asking students how they think the poet feels about the field. How did the poem affect students' feelings?

THIRD ASSIGNMENT
Writing a Response

To help students concretize the ideas and feelings they get from a poem, duplicate and pass out the worksheet on the next page.

Name_____

Writing a Response to a Poem

**Write a response to "Dreams" or "The Old Field."
Here are some ideas to help you get started.**

◆ Write a letter to Langston Hughes. Tell him *your* feelings and ideas about dreams and how to hold fast to them.

◆ Write a poem or story about the old field having a happy time.

◆ In "Dreams," there also is a field, barren and frozen. Write a dialogue in which this field talks to the one in "The Old Field."

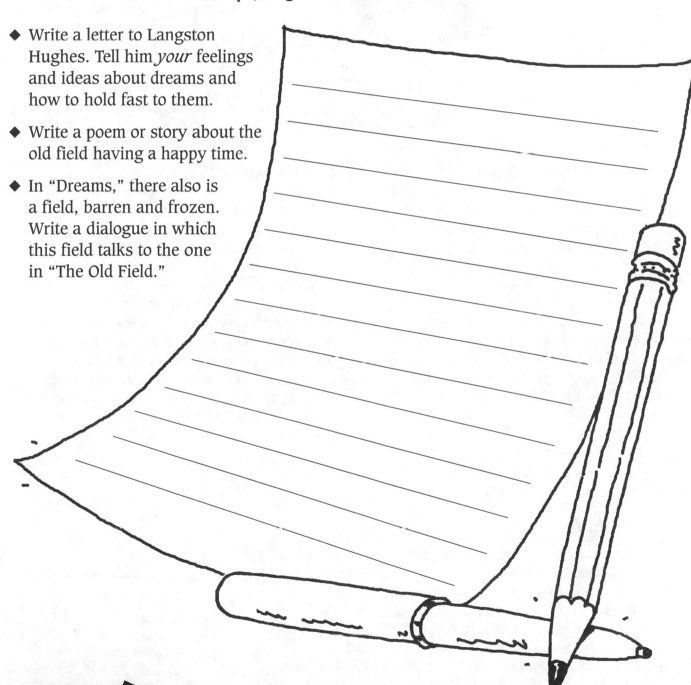

More To Try! ➤ Exchange responses with a partner. Read your partner's work. Then write a response to *that!*

FOURTH ASSIGNMENT
How Does a Poem Mean?

According to the poet John Ciardi, it's not what a poem means, but *how* it means. In this activity students explore two ways, imagery and sound, that poets use to convey meaning.

Imagery

Copy the following poem on the chalkboard or make and distribute copies for each student. You may also wish to display a photo of a seal and its pup. Explain that, just as a field was "thinking" in "The Old Field," a mother seal is speaking in this poem. Before reading the poem aloud, you may also wish to define *combers:* breaking waves; *billow:* a gentle swell in the ocean water; *flipperling:* a baby seal. Ask students to close their eyes as they listen and imagine this lullaby scene.

Seal Lullaby

Oh! hush thee, my baby, the night is behind us,
    And black are the waters that sparkled so green.
The moon, o'er the combers, looks downward to find us
    At rest in the hollows that rustle between.
Where billow meets billow, there soft be thy pillow;
    Ah, weary wee flipperling, curl at thy ease!
The storm shall not wake thee, nor shark overtake thee,
    Asleep in the arms of the slow-swinging seas.

—Rudyard Kipling

From Imagery to Art

Ask students to share the mental pictures that came to them as they listened to the poem. Write their responses on the chalkboard. (Examples: I saw a mother seal folding its flippers around its baby. I saw the mother and baby rocking in the dark water. I saw the moon shining down on the ocean.) Next, ask students to look back at the poem and identify words, phrases, and lines that elicited these mental pictures. Underline these parts of the poem. Then distribute art materials and ask students to draw their mental pictures. As students share their drawings, ask the class to identify details that illustrate the underlined parts of the poem.

Explain that these parts are called *imagery:* words that conjure up pictures in the mind's eye. Encourage students to use this term as they continue to discuss poems.

> **TEACHER TIP**
> You may want to have students look back at the poems on pages 39 and 40 to identify lines that evoke mental pictures.

FIFTH ASSIGNMENT
Listening for Sounds

Point out that lullaby words are supposed to have a gentle, soothing sound. For example, the words *hush thee* are soft and comforting. Ask students to identify other good lullaby words in the poem "Seal Lullaby." *(moon, hollows, billow, pillow, soft, weary, flipperling, slow, and seas)* Invite students to list other words that, all by themselves, sound soft and gentle and lullaby-ish. Examples are *sway, lovely, feather, swish, dreamy,* and *fluffy.*

Write the following poem on the chalkboard and/or make copies to distribute to students. Ask students to listen as you read the poem aloud for words that capture the sighing, moaning sound of the wind. Have students pay particular attention to words with the sound of "ow" as in cow or "oh" as in know. You may wish to point out that the repetition of vowel sounds is called *assonance.*

The Sound of the Wind

The wind has such a rainy sound
    Moaning through the town,
The sea has such a windy sound,
    Will the ships go down?

The apples in the orchard
    Tumble from their tree.
Oh, will the ships go down, go down,
    In the windy sea?

—*Christina Rossetti*

TEACHER TIP
Encourage students to write a lullaby that another animal parent could sing to its baby.

Call on volunteers to read the Rossetti poem aloud, accenting the wind-sound words. Ask listeners to tell what feeling they get as they listen to the poem when these words are accented.

To help students concretize what they've learned about the poetic power of the sounds of words, ask them to write their own poem using the words from one of these lists:

shush	drip	scatter
hush	drop	patter
murmur	drag	flutter
whisper	drizzle	gutter

Discuss how the use of sounds in words adds another layer to the meaning of a poem.

TEACHER TIP
You may also want to use page 67 with this assignment.

What Did We Learn?

In closing, explore these questions with the class. Students may want to write their responses in their scrapbook journals.

1. What are some things that I appreciate about poetry? What do I like best about the poems I have read?

2. How does poetry help me see with "new" eyes?

3. What is something else I would like to learn about poetry?

Writing Poetry

This project offers step-by-step strategies for helping students to write their own poetry.

Getting Started

Before the process of writing can begin, it's important to talk with students about what they think a poem is. Some possible responses:

◆ A poem tells a story.

◆ A poem can rhyme, but it doesn't have to.

◆ A poem is short.

◆ A poem can be about anything.

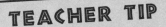

TEACHER TIP

You may want to have students refer to the responses they made about poetry on page 13.

Talking About the Task

It's a good idea to reassure students that when writing a poem, feelings and ideas are important, and sometimes they tumble out so fast it's impossible to worry about spelling or neatness or rhyme. Encourage students to write freely. Spelling and neatness can be fixed later, but a feeling or idea might never come back. Explain that first copies are usually sloppy.

The "Like What" List

The building blocks for poetry writing are similes and metaphors. (See the skills-practice mini-lessons on pages 25–28.) A simple way to present these concepts is in the form of the "Like What" List, which can be posted in the classroom.

How the "Like What" List Works

This list is a reference source. Write it in large letters and hang it in a conspicuous place. Any concept can be taken through the "Like What" List, whether it's concrete (a thing) or abstract (a thought or feeling). For example, the floor may be "tan as a whale's tongue" or "rough like a bumpy road." Peace might be "blue as a glacier in Alaska" or "taste like hot chocolate after a hard day at school."

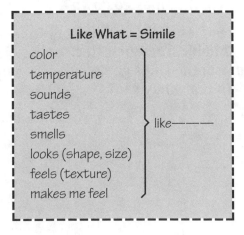

Like What = Simile

color
temperature
sounds
tastes
smells   like———
looks (shape, size)
feels (texture)
makes me feel

_____ is _____ like _____
   (feeling)   (color)

_____

It _____ through/in my _____ like a _____
   (verb)   (room? brain?)

_____

It makes me feel _____ like a _____

_____

OR

It makes me want to _____

FIRST ASSIGNMENT
Feelings

First, brainstorm some feelings with your class and write them on the board, being careful to include a balanced grouping, such as happiness, sadness, boredom, frustration, anger, peace.

Next give students a copy of the poem model above. Explain to the class that a poem model can be changed to suit each student's meaning. For example, students can:

◆ Cross out words they don't need.

◆ Add words of their own where needed.

Next offer a few creative first lines of your own, for example:

◆ "Peace is white like a single snowflake drifting to the ground."

◆ "Boredom is gray as a dull day. It sits on a shelf like a can of cat food waiting to be bought."

◆ "Anger is red like tomato soup bubbling over on the stove."

As Students Write

1. Walk around the room quietly praising and offering encouragement.

2. If you see an interesting poem in progress, ask the child's permission to share it with the class. Nothing inspires more than the children's own writing.

3. Push for details. For example, if a student writes that "Happiness is yellow as a flower," you might ask: "What kind of flower? Where is it? in a vase? on a table? in someone's back-yard?"

TEACHER TIP

Suggest "makes me feel" as a possible ending for poems when an ending is not readily forthcoming. However, be sure students understand that "makes me feel like..." can be used anywhere in a poem.

If a Student Is Stuck

1. Pose more questions. "How do you feel right now? You look frustrated. Perhaps you should write about that. Let's see, what color would your frustration be?"

2. Offer examples that give permission for free thinking. "Hmm. I think frustration is dark like an old cave where a hungry bear just woke up. What do you think?"

3. Offer a different first line to suit the moment and reinforce success rather than failure: "I'm stuck. Stuck is like _____." Ask the student to write about "stuck" things like windows or glue or lollipops in their hair.

Sharing Strategies

It's a good idea to save time at the end of every writing session for sharing, since sharing poems accomplishes many things:

◆ It teaches children that as writers their poems deserve respect, and as readers and listeners they should be respectful of the ideas and feelings of others.

◆ It helps students gain poise in front of a group.

◆ It emphasizes public speaking skills.

Poetry sharing time is both solemn and fun, and no one should be left out (shy children can ask you read their poems until they are ready to do it themselves).

Guessing Game

Here's a sharing variation students never seem to tire of. Collect all the poems and read each without naming the poet. Praise something in the poem and then give the class three chances to guess the author before you reveal his or her name (to applause). This way of sharing is not only fun but also allows students to listen unbiasedly and with no criteria for prior judgment about poems of classmates.

SECOND ASSIGNMENT
"Looking Ats"

"Looking Ats" is another excellent way for students to begin their poetry explorations, because it is grounded in the familiar world of concrete, everyday objects. In this exercise, each child chooses one object to write about, referring to the "Like What" List (see page 44) as a guide to enhance imagery and description.

Pinecones

Some say
they look like pineapples
nestled in green needles.

Some say
they're wearing dragon scales.
This woody fruit
grows up
　　　　or
　　　　　　down
in brown banana
bunches,

clinging to the
summer branches,

waiting.

When at last
the tadpole seedlings burst
to swim the currents
of the wind,

some say
they seem like empty shells

but I say
they are silent bells

with every season's
tale to tell

if we knew
how to listen.

　　　　　　—Jacqueline Sweeney

Prewriting Strategies

Bring to class a picture of a pinecone or, better yet, a bag of pinecones to pass around so students can have a hands-on experience to prompt thinking. After they have had sufficient time to look at and/or touch a pinecone:

◆ Share information about pinecones, offering some descriptive and scientific facts.

◆ Use the "Like What" List to guide a series of questions about shape and color to prompt the verbal formation of similes.

◆ Read the poem on this page, asking students to close their eyes and try to see the pinecone and all of its details as a picture in their minds.

"Pinecones" by Jacqueline Sweeney. Copyright © 1995 by Jacqueline Sweeney. Reprinted by permission of Marian Reiner for the author.

Just Before Writing

Share the following children's poems about objects with students to give them ideas for the writing they're about to do. Discuss the images each poet created. What metaphors and similes did these poets use? How do the poems make students feel about a book bag, frog, and clarinet?

The Clarinet

The clarinet is dark and mysterious like the unknown rivers of Africa.
The clarinet is tall and proud like the graceful towers of France.
The clarinet lifts and carries me, slow and swaying a gentle wind, dancing
through the delicate leaves of a weeping willow, crying for its lost soul.
It takes me to many countries and lands like the frozen soil of the Alaskan tundra.
All of these places are dark, mysterious, tall, proud, slow swaying and gentle
LIKE ME.

—Mulubirhan Kassahun, Grade 5

Frog

The frog's feet are like sticky bubble gum floating through the sky
and the frog's eyes look like eggs burning on the stove and his stomach is like a ball popping in the air.

—Ivan Silva, Grade 4

Book Bag

The Book Bag is rectangular.
It is gray and dirty like my father's socks.
It is a smooth object
with an oval entrance like a mouth waiting to eat my homework.
It reminds me of myself eating.

—Dennis Allen, Grade 6

When It's Time to Write

1. Ask each child to choose any object, animate or inanimate, inside the classroom or outside, something as large as a planet or as small as a dustball under the bed.

2. Next, ask students to close their eyes and look at the objects in their minds.

3. When students have visualized the objects to their satisfaction, ask them to write their object's name on the top of a piece of paper. This is the title of the poem.

4. Refer students to the "Like What" List and ask that they include at least two similes in the description of their objects.

5. Remind them to use their imaginations. If an object is "green like grass," ask them to think of some other green that is surprising and interesting (and not a cliche!), or to give details to make their grass special, such as "green as young grass bent low by a spring breeze."

6. Offer a framework (see page 45) for students having trouble getting started.

Postwriting Strategies

1. Allow students to hear one another's poems. Ask each one to come to the front of the room and read his or her own poem. Show the reader how to develop his or her skills in facing an audience by pausing before reading and waiting for silence if the audience is chatty. This shows children that both poems and readers deserve respect.

2. If time won't allow a formal sharing of poems, you read them. Even if you share a few poems at a time over a period of several days, it will be worth it.

3. Encourage students to illustrate their finished poems and hang them in the classroom or in the hallway for other classes to view.

4. Collaborate with the computer teacher and have your class take their poems to the computer lab where they can type them themselves and possibly illustrate them with computer art.

5. Have a poetry reading for the entire school at an assembly, or have a series of mini-readings where students present their poems to selected groups from other classes.(See also the suggestions on page 20.)

6. Make a booklet of student poems and put it in the library on a designated shelf for all student publications.

7. Have students choose poems to add to their writing portfolios.

What Did We Learn?

To help students think about their writing, explore the following questions with the class.

1. What's the most important thing I learned about writing poetry?

2. Which of my poems do I like best so far? Why?

3. What other kinds of poems would I like to write?

Independent Student Activities and Reproducibles...

...students can use to try a variety of poetry forms

Advice from Poets

What do poets have to say about poetry? What advice do they have for you as a reader and writer of poems? Here are some suggestions from published poets. Some of these you might try right now; you might copy others into your writer's journal for use later on.

1. The Reading Connection
from Mary Ann Hoberman

"I'm going to tell young writers to read, to write things down, and to take their own ideas quite seriously.

"I think one of the greatest things you can do when you're a kid and have such a wonderful memory is to memorize poems—as many as you can."

2. Begin with a Picture
from Nikki Grimes

"Find a picture that you like in a book or magazine, or use a picture that one of your friends drew. Try to imagine what the people in the picture are thinking about or doing. Once you've got a few ideas, make up a poem to match the picture."

3. Close in on Ideas
from Arnold Adoff

"Hold your hands up, shut your eyes, and put your hands close to your nose without touching it. Then open your eyes—that's how close ideas are. Just take pieces of your life and attempt to craft writing out of them."

4. Create a Space
from Shonto Begay

"Have patient eyes and ears. Find a space. Keep it sacred. No TV intrusion, no distraction. A place to create, a place to dream and read."

5. Be Yourself
from Gwendolyn Brooks

"Do not imitate other poets. You are as important as they are.

"Do not be afraid to say something NEW.

"In some of your poems, BE A LITTLE MYSTERIOUS! Surprise yourself and your reader!"

6. Collect Words
from Paul B. Janeczko

"I'm going to tell you one secret to writing poetry: word choice. That is, the job of finding the best words for each line of the poem."

INDEPENDENT STUDENT ACTIVITY / WRITING FROM A MODEL

Rewriting Nursery Rhymes

Nursery rhymes are well-known examples of poems that tell little tales. Like any tale, a nursery rhyme usually has an ending—just think of poor Humpty Dumpty!

As a poet, go wild! Get wacky! *Change* a nursery rhyme to make it read as you imagine it. Here's a nursery rhyme in its usual form:

> Mary had a little lamb,
> Its fleece was white as snow.
> And everywhere that Mary went,
> The lamb was sure to go.
> It followed her to school one day,
> Which was against the rule.
> It made the children laugh and play
> To see the lamb at school.

Here's a *new* version of that rhyme with a few twists and a different ending:

> Mary had a little lamb,
> Its fleece was white as snow.
> But Mary had a wild idea,
> She'd dye the wool Day-Glo!
> She got a pack of lime green dye
> And mixed it in a pool,
> It made the children laugh and play
> To see a lamb so cool!

Think of a nursery rhyme that you know or find one in a book. First write the rhyme in its usual way. Then think of a way to rewrite it. Keep the rhythm and rhyme scheme but add new twists and turns and a new ending. You might want to add extra verses, too.

You can make a two-sided display for your revised rhyme. Fold a sheet of paper in half. Cut out a shape along the fold so that when you open it, you see two mirror-image shapes. Make them big enough to fit the poems. Write the "real" version on one side of the shape and your version on the other. Post the shape on a bulletin board so that readers can compare the Before and After versions.

Writing to Form

Some poetry doesn't rhyme. Still, it may have a special form the poet follows to shape an idea, a feeling, or an experience. Two forms of unrhymed poetry are haiku *(HIGH-coo) and* cinquain *(SIN-kane).*

Here's Haiku

Haiku is a Japanese form of unrhymed poetry, usually about nature. It is a short, delicate poem about a single idea. Favorite haiku topics include flowers, trees, animals, seasons, and weather. Haiku always has three lines and a total of 17 syllables. Read this haiku to understand its form:

Warm April sunrise—	5 syllables
Tender green shoots pierce the soil,	7 syllables
Aiming for the sun.	5 syllables

A good way to get a feel for writing haiku is to read some. Japanese poet Basho, who lived over three hundred years ago, is famous for developing the haiku form. Look for haiku by Basho in the library, or read haiku in collections such as *Don't Tell the Scarecrow and Other Japanese Poems* by Issa and Others.

Create your own haiku about nature. Follow the form on this page. When you become familiar with writing haiku, you might experiment with the form. For example, shift the number of syllables per line, as long as the total is 17 and the second line is the longest. Display your haiku by writing it on paper and placing it and a leaf or flower between two sheets of clear contact paper.

Cinquain Structure

Cinq (pronounced "sank") is the French word for five, which is how many lines a cinquain has. Like haiku, cinquain has a form that counts lines and syllables. But unlike haiku, a cinquain can be about anything, and each line presents a certain idea.

Idea	Syllables	Cinquain
Topic	2	**Chorus**
Description of the topic	4	**Many voices**
Actions that fit the topic	6	**Creating harmony**
Feelings about the topic	8	**Joyous, hopeful, graceful, dreamy**
Another word for the topic	2	**Music**

Try a cinquain. A good way to start is to think of a topic and another word for it. Use these for your first and fifth lines. Then work on the middle lines. Remember to think about the number of syllables and the purpose of each line. After you make your first draft, read your cinquain to a classmate. Adjust the words as needed to make the best cinquain you can.

Mishmash and Balderdash!

**Some poems make no sense.
These are called nonsense rhymes.**

Nonsense Syllables

Many poems are fun to hear and say because they contain nonsense words or syllables. Here are some lines from poems that include nonsense words:

Hey <u>diddle</u>, <u>diddle</u>,
the cat and the fiddle...

My hen went
"<u>Shimmy-shack,
shimmy-shack</u>..."

<u>Knick-knack</u>, <u>paddy-whack</u>,
give a dog a bone...

Make up some nonsense words or syllables that are fun to say. Use them in poems about silly subjects.

This Poem Makes No Sense!

Sometimes a whole poem is nonsense! Here's an example:

Once was a man named Michael Finnegan,
He grew whiskers on his chinnegan,
Along came a wind and blew them innegan,
Poor old Michael Finnegan—begin again!
[Repeat the verse.]

Discuss these questions about the poem with a partner or in a group:

1. What nonsense do you notice in the topic of the poem?

2. What nonsense do you notice in the language of the poem?

3. What nonsense do you notice in the structure of the poem?

Think of a ridiculous situation, a foolish mix of characters, or any silly subject for a poem. Make it rhyme. If you wish, include nonsense syllables or silly words that are fun to say out loud. Present your nonsense poem to classmates or to younger children. You might even work with a group to plan a nonsense poetry reading for a kindergarten or first-grade class in your school. Ask your teacher for suggestions on how to organize this event.

Name_____

Laugh with a Limerick

Do you like to laugh? Then a limerick is a poem for you.
A limerick is a short, funny poem with five lines.

Study the limerick on this page. Then follow
the model to write a limerick of your own.

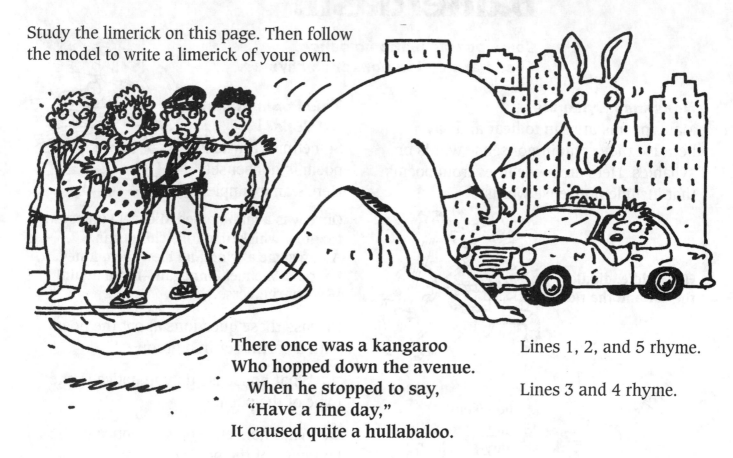

There once was a kangaroo
Who hopped down the avenue.
    When he stopped to say,
    "Have a fine day,"
It caused quite a hullabaloo.

Lines 1, 2, and 5 rhyme.

Lines 3 and 4 rhyme.

There once was a _____

Who _____

_____

_____

_____

More to Try! Illustrate your limerick.

56

Name_____

Poems Take Shape

A concrete poem is one that's shaped like its subject matter. Here's an example.

Now it's your turn. In BOX 1, create a short concrete poem about an umbrella. To get inspired, shut your eyes and imagine that you *are* an umbrella. How does the rain sound? Are you soaked? Are you lonely? When you're finished, use BOX 2 to design a concrete poem in a shape you choose.

PIZZA PIZZAZZ
Have you ever seen a more delicious sight,
than a pizza dressed up to go out at night?
Thick tomato sauce and mozzarella cheese,
mushrooms, sausage, more peppers, please!
Onions, olives, choice / pepperoni!
Anything goes, just / hold the anchovies!
Top it all off with a / sprinkle of spice—
it's looking so / good…
Hey, who / took a slice?

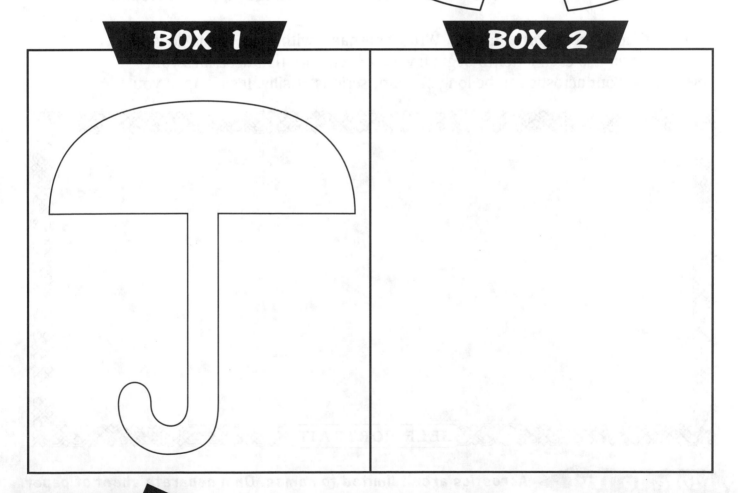

BOX 1

BOX 2

More To Try! Look for other examples of concrete poems in books of poetry.

57

Name _____

What's in a Name?

An *acrostic* is a poem in which the first letter of each line forms a word when it's read from top to bottom. Here are two acrostics about people:

Many hopes, many dreams.
Able to make awesome oatmeal cookies.
Totally into my dog Jordan and basketball.
The Chicago Bull's #1 fan, that's me!

Sensitive, shy, stubborn, quiet, careful.
Artistic, athletic, great at keeping secrets.
Really likes gymnastics, sad movies, shopping,
And my best friends in the world: Tia and Kate.
Has a passion for cats and fudge-ripple ice cream.

Now it's time to toot *your* own horn. Write your name within the frame down the left side. Then use each letter to begin a word or sentence that describes your personality. Your acrostic can be long or short, serious or silly. It's all up to you!

> ### SELF-PORTRAIT

More To Try! ▶ Acrostics aren't limited to names. On a separate sheet of paper, try writing one that honors a place such as Texas, a color such as purple, or an underappreciated object such as your pencil!

Name_____

Haiku + Ageku = Tanka

Like haiku, *tanka* is form of Japanese unrhymed poetry. A tanka starts out with a haiku, then has two more lines called *ageku*. A poet can use the ageku to add a personal response to the haiku or to create a fuller thought. Here's an example of a tanka. Notice the number of syllables in each line.

Sparrows chirp sweetly	5 syllables
To welcome the spring sunrise,	7 syllables
Disturbing my dream.	5 syllables
Weary, I stretch, rub my eyes	7 syllables
I'm not yet ready to sing.	7 syllables

} haiku
} ageku

Write a tanka of your own. Use this form to help you.

} haiku

} ageku

More To Try! → Take a haiku you've already written. Add an ageku to it to create a tanka.

Name_____

Your Turn with a Lanterne

A lanterne is a five-line poem. Can you tell where this poem gets its name?

Our — 1 syllable
dizzy — 2 syllables
gray kitten — 3 syllables
plays hide and seek. — 4 syllables
Boo! — 1 syllable

Read the sample lanterne. Each line has a specific number of syllables. Notice that the lines do not rhyme.

Write your own lanterne in the space provided.

_____

_____

_____

_____

_____

More To Try! Cut out your lanterne, tie a piece of yarn through the top, and display the poem in your classroom.

Name_____

LITERATURE LINK

Super Sentences

A poem that's only a sentence long can tell a rich and wonderful story. Take a look at this:

The Red Ball

The red ball
slipped from
the baby's hands
bounced,
bounced,
bounced,
down the cement stairs,
zoomed past
the fire hydrant,
raced through
a championship game
of hopscotch,
crossed the street,
rolled under
a blue car,
then zigzagged between
two dozen pairs
of feet,
until one sneaker
kicked it up
into the air
with such force
it landed
with a PLUNK!
in the tidy nest
of a jay—
who, by the way,
is still waiting
for the curious egg
to hatch.

"The Red Ball" is only one sentence long, but it takes the reader on a colorful journey. Now it's your turn. Write a sentence poem in the box below. (If you like, draft your poem on another sheet of paper.) Your sentence poem can be about a raindrop, the wind, a secret—even the gum on the bottom of someone's shoe!

More To Try!

Try writing a *sentence riddle poem.* Here's how: Describe an object or a person in one sentence. You might want to begin your poem, *I am...* Challenge classmates to find the answer.

"The Red Ball" by Liza Charlesworth

61

Recognizing Rhythm

Rhythm is an important part of poetry. These activities can help you get a better idea about what rhythm is and how it works in poetry.

What Is Rhythm?

Imagine the sound of a horse galloping. "Listen" for the strongest part of the hoof beats. Now say each of these words out loud: *lion, elephant, kangaroo.* Which word has that galloping feel?

Rhythm in poetry comes from the way words are chosen and combined. We feel *accents* (strong beats) in words. Read the words below and notice how your head moves to indicate the accent.

Words with	Examples
accent in the <u>beginning</u>	*onion, lovely, peanuts, Mexico*
accent at the <u>end</u>	*garage, Jamaal, forget, amaze*
accent in the <u>middle</u>	*potato, important, Melissa, Chicago*
<u>two</u> accents	*information, celebration, Alabama, Oklahoma*

Work with a partner to brainstorm words for each rhythmic pattern. Can you think of five examples for each? Does your name fit one of the patterns? Which one?

Lyrics

Some songs are really poems set to music. *Lyrics,* or the words of a song, are written so that the rhythm of the tune and accents of the words fit together. Consider these lyrics:

This land is your land, this land is my land,
From California to the New York island,
From the redwood forests to the Gulf
   Stream waters,
This land was made for you and me.

What would happen if the places in the second line were changed to *From Texas to Block Island?* Try singing these "new" words. What happens?

Think of lyrics to a song you know. Write them out as if they were a poem. Then highlightthe words (or syllables) that get accents. Draw vertical lines with a pencil to show where the main beats are, or the places where you might clap to keep time. For example:

|Jingle |bells, |jingle |bells,
|Jingle |all the |way, |
|Oh what |fun it |is to |ride
On a |one-horse |open |sleigh! |

Try this at home. Listen to songs you like on the radio or on tapes or CDs. Notice how the lyrics rhyme and where the accents are.

Challenge

Write new lyrics to a song you already know. This is called a *parody,* especially when the new lyrics are funny. Write the lyrics to fit the rhythm of the original. Present your new lyrics by singing them to classmates or by recording them on audiotape.

INDEPENDENT STUDENT ACTIVITY / ACTIVITY POEM—RHYTHM

A Poem To Sink Your Teeth Into

Here's a poem that's good enough to eat! Read through the list of ingredients, then sing the rest of the poem to "She'll Be Coming 'Round the Mountain"! To create a yummy batch of cookies, follow the directions to the letter. Be sure to yell as you stir the mixture.

Nutty Chocolate Cookies

Preheat oven to 375 degrees.
You will need: bowl, stirring spoon, greased cookie sheet, measuring cups and spoons, teaspoon

¾ cup brown sugar, firmly packed
½ teaspoon baking soda
1½ cups flour
2 tablespoons water
1 egg
½ cup shortening
1 teaspoon salt
½ cup chopped nuts
1 cup chocolate bits

Mix to the tune of "She'll Be Coming 'Round the Mountain":

Cream the shortening with the sugar, cream it well.
Stir the mixture with a spoon, now give a yell.
Add the flour to the bowl;
Add the egg as you are told.
Stir the mixture with a spoon and add the salt.

Mix the soda with the water, mix it well;
Add the mixture to the bowl, now give a yell.
Add the nuts and chocolate bits;
Stir as if you're having fits.
Stir the mixture in the bowl, as you are told.

Take a teaspoon of the mixture and be neat.
Drop it carefully upon a cookie sheet.
Now repeat until you clean up;
Bake the cookies till they brown up.
Bake the cookies till they brown up—fit to eat.

Bake 10 to 12 minutes. Makes 30 cookies.

—Pauline Watson

"Nutty Chocolate Cookies" from *Cricket's Cookery* by Pauline Watson and the Editors of *Cricket* magazine. Reprinted by permission of *Cricket* magazine.

The Singing Cook

Whip up your own favorite recipe to the tune of another familiar rhyming song. Possibilities include "On Top of Old Smokey," "Mister Frog Went A-Courting," "The Farmer in the Dell," and "Row, Row, Row Your Boat." For other inspirations, check *The Fireside Book of Children's Songs* edited by Marie Winn (Simon and Schuster, 1966) or other songbooks in your library.

A Poetry Eat-In

Lots of poems are about food. One especially yummy anthology with poems selected by William Cole is titled Poem Stew (Harper, 1981). Work with a group to collect food poems that are "good enough to eat." Then plan a pot-luck feast where everyone brings a dish that goes with one of the poems. Spread out the goodies and alternate eating with reading aloud your tasty poetry.

Cat Hat, Mouse House

Many poems rhyme, while others don't. If you choose to use rhyme in a poem, here are some rhyme patterns you can play with.

Pattern 1: Two by Two

You can make pairs of lines rhyme, as in the poem below.

Storm

Wind growls.	(a)
Wind prowls.	(a)
Gust batters.	(b)
Gust clatters.	(b)
Breeze brushes.	(a)
Breeze shushes.	(a)
Peace falls.	(b)
Sleep calls.	(b)

Can you guess what the letters in parentheses stand for at the end of the lines? Here's a hint: They relate to the words that rhyme.

Now, write your own *aabb* poem about weather and wind.

Pattern 2: Skip-Skip

Int the poem "The Dawn Wind," find the a rhymes and the b rhymes. Write or say the rhyming words in the order they appear.

The Dawn Wind

At two o'clock in the morning, if you open your window and listen,
You will hear the feet of the wind that is going to call the sun.
And the trees in the shadow rustle and the trees in the moonlight glisten,
And though it is deep, dark night, you feel that the night is done.

—*Rudyard Kipling*

The rhyme pattern in "The Dawn Wind" is called *abab*.
If you can figure out why, you're ready to write your own *abab* poem.

Make Up Some Rhyme Patterns of Your Own

You can be playful with poetry. One way is to create rhyme patterns of your own.

An abba pattern:

The moon is bright.
A star glows.
Little towns doze
Through the friendly night.

An abcb pattern:

The moon shines.
The stars are bright.
Sleepers dream
In a blanket of light.

Make up a rhyme pattern. Jot down some lines for a poem. See if you can make your poem fit the pattern. If the pattern doesn't fit your ideas and word pictures, change to a pattern that does fit them. Remember that ideas and images are the most important parts of poems. Rhyme is what you add later, if you want.

Poetry Around the Calendar

Poets often find ideas by observing the changing seasons. Here is how the poet Oliver Herford expressed his feelings about a winter moment.

I Heard a Bird Sing

I heard a bird sing
In the dark of December
A magical thing
And sweet to remember:
"We are nearer to Spring
Than we were in September,"
I heard a bird sing
In the dark of December.

—*Oliver Herford*

Diamante

A diamante (dee-uh-MAHN-tay) is an unrhymed seven-line poem. It has the shape of a diamond, which is what diamante means. In a *diamante,* a poet compares two opposite ideas. The diamante below is about opposite seasons—winter and summer. Notice how the rules of each line help the poet make contrasts.

Create a diamante about opposite seasons. Make the poem show the contrasts between the opposites. Display your diamantes on diamond-shaped paper.

WINTER

frosty, bitter

shivering, huddling, slipping

icicle, scarf, surfboard, bicycle

swimming, laughing, riding

steamy, lazy

SUMMER

1 word—
names the first subject

2 words—
describe the subject

3 -*ing* words about the subject

4 words—2 about the subject,
2 about the opposite subject

3 -*ing* words about the opposite subject

2 words—
describe the opposite subject

1 word—
names the opposite subject

Calendar Colors

Images can create moods and impressions about the seasons. What senses do the following images stir up?

May is lavender—
A sprays of lilacs

August is yellow—
Butter melting on sweet corn

Write a brief image of your own for each month of the year. Follow this form:

[Month] is [color]—
[an idea for the color and season]

When you have images for all twelve months, use them to make a poetry calendar. Or, as a group, combine images about the same months or seasons.

Poetry from a Painting

What do painting and poetry have in common? More than meets the eye! Both are creative expressions. Both present an artist or writer's unique view of the world.

To the right is a famous picture called *The Starry Night.* It was made by Dutch painter Vincent van Gogh in 1889. It is his vision of a village under the evening sky. Do you think the painting shows reality or fantasy? The answer is both. Yes, there are hills, bushes, and houses; and the moon and stars are in the sky where they belong. But—wait a minute!—those stars are really, really bright and really, really big. And they seem to be swirling across the sky. That's because van Gogh let his feelings, as well as his eyes, guide his paintbrush.

Poets do much the same thing. Instead of brushstrokes and color, they use words to paint their pictures. For example, one famous poet spoke of the stars that "glitter like a swarm of fireflies tangled in a silver braid."

Look at *The Starry Night.* How would you describe the scene that van Gogh painted? Jot down the words that come to your mind when you look at it. Then try to "step inside the painting" and write a short poem that *really* describes it. Or close your eyes and use your own memory of a starry night to create a poem. Remember, poetry doesn't have to rhyme or be realistic—it just has to express *your* unique feelings.

When you're finished, exchange poems with a friend. How are your poems alike? Different? Would an artist illustrate your poems in the same way? Why or why not?

Vincent van Gogh. *The Starry Night* (1889). Oil on canvas, 29 × 36¼ in. (73.7 × 92.1 cm). The Museum of Modern Art, New York. Acquired through the Lillie P. Bliss Bequest. Photograph © 1995 The Museum of Modern Art, New York.

Say It Your Way

As a poet, you have many choices to make. For example, after choosing a subject, you can choose the way you want to tell about it. Will your poem be funny or serious? Will it be a riddle poem, a haiku, a cinquain, or a limerick? Will your poem tell a story? Paint a word picture? Express your feelings? Here are three ways three different poets tell about the subject of *whistling.*

When I Learned To Whistle

I remember the day when I learned to whistle,
It was in Spring and new sounds were all around.
I was five or six and my front teeth were missing,
But I blew until my cheeks stuck out.

I remember walking up and down the block,
Trying to impress those that heard me
With the tunes and sounds that came from my mouth,
For I sounded much better than the birds in the trees.

I remember being hurt, for nobody seemed to care,
And then I met an old man who stopped and smiled.
He too blew until his cheeks stuck out.
He sounded just like me, for his front teeth were missing.

—*Gordon Lea, Age 11*

Just a Couple of Notes

Tasty Tune

My lips pursed up like the sour of lemons.
But the sound came out like the sweetness of pears.

Different Voices

1. Get together with five or six classmates. Decide on a sound you can all write a poem about, such as the sound of drums, rain, squeaky shoes, or sloshing washing machines.

2. Review or explore the poetry forms and ideas in this unit.

3. On your own, write a poem about the sound your group chose.

4. Meet with your group again. Share and compare the different poems you all wrote. Discuss how the poems are alike and different.

5. Finally, discuss what you learned about poetry from this activity.

Teacher's Notebook...

...including tips on technology and assessment, and a bibliography

Bits and Bytes

No matter what techniques students use to create their poetry, some high- and low-tech ideas can enhance the presentation of their works.

> ## TEACHER TIP
> Create a class poetry anthology using the most convenient method your school provides for making multiple copies. Encourage students to submit their favorite poems. Have a collating party to put the books together.

Printed Presentations

◆ Most word-processing software allows users to highlight words in **boldface** or in *italics.* Invite student poets to use either of these styles to call attention to onomatopoeia, to indicate rhymes, or to feature nonsense syllables.

◆ Most software lets users center an entire paragraph or a single line. This is a useful feature for printing diamantes, lanternes, or some concrete poems.

> ## TEACHER TIP
> Have students write their concrete poems on transparencies, which makes them easy to share with the class on the overhead projector.

◆ Some software allows users to create a dropped capital letter (also known as a display capital letter). This technique can be used to highlight an acrostic poem or any verse in which students want to call out the first word.

◆ If you have access to a color printer, encourage students to select colors that best suit the text.

Software Suggestions

Poetry in Motion is CD-ROM software that offers video performances, interviews, and original texts by twenty-three poets. Students can see and hear how "real" poets talk about and read their works.

Zillion Kajillion Rhymes is a rhyming dictionary for the computer, available for both Macintosh or IBM systems. Students can use this software to help them find rhymes for ordinary words, as well as for place names, product names, and scientific terms.

> ## TEACHER TIP
> Make an audio- or videotape recording of a poetry reading in which each student selects and presents his or her best work. Show the completed tape at an open house event, send it around the class on revolving home loan, or add it to the school library collection for posterity!

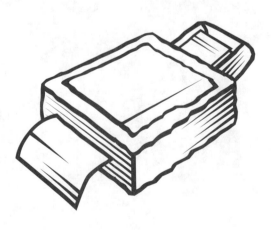

Portfolios and Presentations

Poetry and Portfolios

As students pen their poems, encourage them to make revisions until they think their poems sound and feel just right. To help students see progress in their work, have them keep drafts together in a poetry folder. Be sure students reflect in writing on each draft before moving on to the next. (See page 36 for a reproducible students can refer to on the revision process.) Add these draft series to students' portfolios to show process and growth.

Guiding Assessment

Because poetry encourages students to communicate inner thoughts and feelings, sometimes a risky business, it's important that assessment focus on the positive. As you conference with children about their poems, you can use questions to increase children's awareness of the techniques they already use as well as help them identify areas they'd like to work on.

◆ What senses do you focus on in your poem?

◆ If you use rhyme, which words rhyme?

◆ What are some of the comparisons you make in your poem?

◆ How do your words express a feeling?

◆ How do you create a musical feeling in your poem? (Alliteration: Do you hear words that begin with similar sounds? Repetition: Are there lines that begin with the same word or words? Consonance: Do you repeat any sounds at the ends of your words?)

Presentation Possibilities

Sharing is an important part of the poetry-writing process. Students benefit from opportunities to share something as personal as poetry with a supportive audience. It's natural, too, that children will pay extra attention to content and technique when sharing—letting you better evaluate what they're really capable of and in which areas you might offer reinforcement lessons. Here are some ways to share poetry. (See pages 16 and 20 for other ideas.)

Poetry Readings Children can read aloud original poems, dramatize them, or set them to music or dance. You might organize a poetry reading. Videotape individual presentations for students' portfolios if possible.

Tape-Recorded Readings Students might read aloud a poem on cassette, playing it for an audience or sharing it at the poetry center.

Poetry Displays Students can showcase their work in displays they create for a classroom, library, or other school space.

Poetry Pals Consider exchanging students' poetry with a class in another school. If you have access to an on-line service, you can E-mail poetry back and forth, even create a shared anthology of student work.

Poetry Magazine Invite students to select a best poem for publication in a class or school magazine.

Answers to Student Worksheets: p. 13: Responses will vary. **p. 28:** Similes and metaphors will vary. **p. 32:** 1. big pig 2. new glue 3. bright light 4. red shed 5. cheap jeep 6. dull skull 7. lunch hunch 8. top cop 9. blue moo 10. float coat **p. 41:** Responses will vary. **p. 56:** Limericks will vary. Check that students' limericks follow the correct rhyme pattern. **p. 57:** Concrete poems will vary. **p. 58:** Acrostic poems will vary. Check that acrostic words are spelled correctly. **p. 59:** Tankas will vary. Check that students' tankas follow the correct syllable pattern. **p. 60:** Lanternes will vary. Check that students' lanternes follow the correct syllable pattern. **p. 61:** Sentence poems will vary.

Bibliography

Poetry

Agave Blooms Just Once by Gisela Jernigan (Harbinger House)

All the Small Poems and Fourteen More by Valerie Worth (Farrar, Straus & Giroux)

Beast Feast and Bing Bang Boing by Douglas Florian (Harcourt)

Casey at the Bat by Ernest Lawrence Thayer (Putnam)

Cowboys by Charles Sullivan (Rizzoli)

Dancing Teepees selected by Virginia Driving Hawk Sneve (Holiday House)

The Earth Is Painted Green edited by Barbara Brenner (Scholastic)

Favorite Poems Old and New selected by Helen Ferris (Doubleday)

Growltiger's Last Stand by T. S. Eliot (Farrar, Straus & Giroux)

Hailstones and Halibut Bones and *Fingers Are Always Bringing Me News* by Mary O'Neill (Doubleday)

I'm Nobody! Who Are You? by Emily Dickinson (Stemmer House)

Long Ago in Oregon by Claudia Lewis (Harper)

Make a Joyful Sound: Poems for Children by African-American Poets edited by Deborah Slier (Checkerboard Press)

Mother Gave a Shout: Poems by Women and Girls edited by Susanna Steele and Morag Styles (Volcano Press)

The New Kid on the Block by Jack Prelutsky (Greenwillow)

A New Treasury of Children's Poetry selected by Joanna Cole (Doubleday)

The Nonsense Verse of Edward Lear by Edward Lear (Harmony)

Paul Revere's Ride by Henry Wadsworth Longfellow (Greenwillow)

The Poetry Break by Caroline Feller Bauer (H.W. Wilson)

Poetry Place Anthology (Scholastic)

The Random House Book of Poetry for Children edited by Jack Prelutsky

Side by Side: Poems to Read Together collected by Lee Bennett Hopkins (Simon and Schuster)

Sing a Song of Popcorn edited by Beatrice Schenk de Regniers (Scholastic)

Space Songs and Celebrations by Myra Cohn Livingston (Scholastic)

Street Music by Arnold Adoff (Harper)

A Swinger of Birches by Robert Frost (Stemmer House)

Talking to the Sun selected by Kenneth Koch and Kate Farell (Holt)

This Same Sky edited by Naomi Shihab Nye (Four Winds Press)

Trees by Harry Behn (Holt)

Winter Poems selected by Barbara Rogasky (Scholastic)

Where the Sidewalk Ends and *A Light in the Attic* by Shel Silverstein (Harper)

Nonfiction

The Scholastic Rhyming Dictionary by Sue Young

Teacher Resources

Quick Poetry Activities You Can Really Do and *Teaching Poetry: Yes You Can!* by Jacqueline Sweeney (Scholastic)

Reading and Writing Poetry: A Guide for Teachers by Judith Steinbergh (Scholastic)